T0124171

The Ultimate Guide
for Women to Understand
MEN

By Alex and Elizabeth Lluch

WS Publishing Group
San Diego, California

The Ultimate Guide
for Men & Women to
Understand Each Other

The Ultimate Guide for Women to Understand Men

By Alex and Elizabeth Lluch
Published by WS Publishing Group
San Diego, California 92119
Copyright © 2010 by WS Publishing Group

All rights reserved under International and Pan-American Copyright conventions. No part of this book may be reproduced or transmitted in any form or by any means, electronic or mechanical, including photocopy, recording or by any information storage and retrieval system, without permission in writing from the publisher.

Designed by WS Publishing Group:
David Defenbaugh, Sarah Jang

Image Credit: Sandals: © iStockphoto/Skip ODonnell

For Inquiries:
Log on to www.WSPublishingGroup.com
E-mail info@WSPublishingGroup.com

ISBN: 978-1-934386-86-6
This book is part of a two-book set.
Not to be sold separately

Printed in China

Table of Contents

Table of Contents

Introduction

In 2008, Michael Kimmel, a professor of sociology and gender studies at the State University of New York at Stony Brook, published *Guyland: The Perilous World Where Boys Become Men*. In it, Kimmel claims that men ages 16 to 26 exist in a directionless, adolescent limbo called "Guyland."

Men that reside in Guyland refuse to grow up and, as a result, are unmarried and have low-paying or entry level jobs. They often live with roommates, in fraternity-like houses, or even at home with their parents. They tend to indulge in frequent, non-monogamous sex and pornography, are prone to pranks, violence, and homophobia, and have episodes of binge drinking and drug use. They spend money frivolously, and are filled with a sense of foiled entitlement and chronic dissatisfaction that prevents them from ever wanting to take on adult responsibilities—especially marriage.

Women reading this guide to their mate may recognize their own complaints about their partners in much of the Guyland criteria. Indeed, the single most common complaint women have about men is that they refuse to grow up. And though there are many reasons for why this may be true, the answer may partly reside in the emerging idea that today's men lack the role models and scenarios to prepare them for healthy, successful, and mature relationships.

Kimmel interviewed hundreds of young men and found the majority (though not all) were white, middle-class, angry, disillusioned, and one step away from a serious violent backlash against a society they felt had disempowered them. The men in his study believed they had been overtaken by women on the job and in salary level. They also felt women had invaded sports, bars, firehouses, and other traditionally male haunts, and even that institutions that previously had a typical male bent—such as food or comedy—had been feminized. Finally, they described feeling villainized and victimized by a growing class of minorities whose demand for equal rights overshadowed their own.

These men felt pushed out of their place in society by women and other underrepresented groups. As a result, they had little idea how to transition from boyhood to manhood since so many of their ideas about masculinity were tied to being large and in charge. Without a sense of power, these young men resorted to their basest instincts, formed fraternal groups, and policed each other's gendered characteristics through bullying and homophobic humor.

The Impact of Divorce on Today's Men

The story of how these kind of boys grew into these kind of men actually begins back in 1960, when only 2.2 of every 1,000 marriages ended in divorce. This meant that most kids were growing up in two-parent homes. Indeed, the American family of the early 1960s most often had a dad who worked and a mom who stayed home with the children. In those days, only about a third of women worked outside the home—68 percent of women stayed put. Boys raised during this time had fathers that primarily worked such masculine job as machine operators and craftsmen. Furthermore, according to the U.S. Bureau of Labor Statistics, the average head of household was male, 48 years old, and had an eleventh grade education. This generation of fathers either encouraged their sons to go to college to do better than they had, or passed down proprietorship of their family business, proving college was not a necessity. Either way, their boys were groomed to succeed and were taught the world was theirs for the taking.

When the Women's Liberation Movement began to get a foothold in the mid-to-late 1960s, however, the divorce rate started to steadily increase. It peaked in 1981, when the number of divorces more than doubled to 5.3 out of every 1,000 marriages. The U.S. Census Bureau reports that 86 percent of single parents at that time were women, a trend which continued into the 1990s. As a result, young men born in the 1980s found themselves being raised by their single, working mothers. They became part of the growing number of regular daycare and latchkey kids known as Generation Y—many of the boys and men you are currently dating or married to.

Many of these boys grew up with weekend-only or absentee fathers—and with moms that felt guilty for working so much. Divorced moms and dads treated their latchkey kids to lots and lots of "stuff," like new toys, video games, sports equipment, and even computers to keep them company during the long hours they spent home alone after school. Being raised by technology became one reason why the boys of Generation Y became, as American author Eric Chester has described them, "impatient, desensitized, disengaged, skeptical, disrespectful, [and] bluntly expressive." In addition, their ideas about masculinity and what it means to be a man were shaped by different forces than previous generations.

Proponents of conservative family values tend to blame

single mothers for changing the way their sons perceived masculinity. They argue it is not natural for women to be head of household and that presenting women in this way confuses boys about masculinity. Others argue that absentee fathers and deadbeat dads are to blame. By dropping out of their sons' lives after divorce, they say a boy's only option for learning how to be a man is their mother. Many of these mothers were often so overworked, underpaid, and stressed, they barely had time to check homework, let alone find appropriate male role models. Regardless of who is to blame, the boys of Generation Y did not get to view gender roles through the clearly focused binoculars of the 1950s and '60s. Instead, their view of gender is more of a kaleidoscope filled with changing images and mixed messages about what it means to be a man.

"I Am Man, Now Leave Me Alone"

As children of divorce with uncertain gender roles, most Generation Y boys transitioned into men just as the new millennium hit. In the time they grew up, technology had taken giant leap. With computers in 76 percent of homes by 2003, nearly everyone outfitted with cell phones, and extremely realistic video games, Gen Y became the first generation to be plugged in all the time. As a result, they became accustomed to instant gratification—and an endless supply of online possibilities, from watching college pranks on YouTube.com to viewing porn. With the constant thrill of variety at their fingertips, it became very difficult for these guys to imagine themselves ever settling down or getting married.

According to the U.S. Census Bureau, in the early 1960s the average man got married when he was 22 years old. In the 1980s it was 24, and in 2003 the average age had jumped to just over 27. This jives with Michael Kimmel's research, who found that 27 is about the age when men exit Guyland and finally take the plunge into adult manhood. Women who date men residing in this period of extended adolescence may experience a lot of frustration as they attempt to get their boyfriends to grow up, move out of their parents' basements, and take the plunge into marriage. Women who date men in their early-to-mid 20s are often met with such resistance to marriage that they resort to ultimatums, such as threatening to break up or find a man who actually wants to get married. Such women are confused by their boyfriend's behavior and conclude their boyfriend doesn't want them, when in reality he doesn't know what he wants because he is not ready to think about it yet.

But most men do want to get married—they just don't want to be rushed or forced into it. A report issued by the National Marriage Project at Rutgers University found that the majority of men plan to get married at some point, but not until they feel it is time to settle down. David Popenoe, co-author of the Rutgers study, advises women to snag their guy at this critical time. Though 27 is the average age at which men "feel ready," it may seem like some men will never get to that point. Hence the relationship battle between the sexes ensues: she wants him to commit; he wants her to wait and see what happens.

Women might better serve their marital agenda by learning to recognize the signs that their boyfriends are perched to become husbands. Signs he's thinking about taking the next step include:

1. He goes out to bars less often with the guys, and says he'd rather go out with you.
2. He brings up marriage and wanting to have a family.
3. You have met his friends and family on more than one occasion.
4. He gets a real job and opens a savings account.
5. He lets you keep stuff at his apartment.
6. He frequently tells you he loves you.

Instead of trying to change him to fit your timeline, seek out indications that he's graduated from Guyland and is getting ready to grow up and settle down. Otherwise, you set yourself up for a battle of wills that you probably will not win. Indeed, the more you try to force a man to do anything, the more he is likely to resist.

The Ultimate Guide for Women to Understand Men will help you unravel your partner's complexities by providing straightforward scenarios with well-researched advice for how to peel back his emotional layers and find out what's really going on. By employing the techniques outlined in each of the six chapters, you will come closer to understanding not only your boyfriend or husband, but all of the men in your life.

Commitment
& Fidelity

In 1920 Sigmund Freud published the essay "Beyond the Pleasure Principle" in which he discussed his theory that the human psyche could be broken down into three components: the id, the ego, and the super-ego.

The id seeks instant gratification and pleasure; the super-ego strives for perfection and serves as the conscience; and the ego acts as a reality check that regulates thoughts and desires and prevents either the id or super-ego from taking over completely. One way to gain an understanding of your mate is to consider which of Freud's psychic components seems to drive your partner's personality.

If your partner is driven by his id, he is likely very immature, jealous, controlling, demanding, and irrational. His desire for commitment is based on immediate pleasure, rather than long-term investment. You may even describe him as infantile—an accurate label since Freud believed newborns were ruled by the id. Trying to please a partner this selfish is impossible, because he will never be satisfied with what he has. On the other hand, a man ruled by the super-ego is probably repressed, guilt-ridden, has low self-esteem, and is not much fun at all. He is likely obsessed with proper etiquette and more concerned with how things appear than their actual substance. His expectations for himself and his partner are so high that neither he, nor she can possibly meet them.

Figure out why he does what he does:

1. He is jealous because he does not want to share his greatest pleasure—you—with another man.

2. He wants you to settle down and demonstrate your loyalty because he has definitive ideas about what a relationship should look, feel, and act like.

3. He doesn't want you to flirt or become too close to male friends, because he is a realist, and he knows what can happen when chemistry develops between men and women.

Contrary to popular opinion, therefore, dating a man with a huge ego is the best possible version of Freud's psychic model. A man driven by his ego is realistic, even-tempered, fun-loving, responsible, dedicated, hard-working, loyal, faithful, and committed—so hang on to him, and learn to encourage these qualities in your partner.

Kick Flirting to the Curb

He is threatened by other men's overtures. It is important to show your loyalty by refraining from flirting when you're out with him.

The Scenario
You flirt with bartenders, waiters, and even old male friends on Facebook. It's all meaningless to you, but this behavior seriously threatens your partner's trust threshold. Learn why this bothers him and how giving up your flirty ways will improve your relationship.

Situation at a Glance
- He becomes sullen and snaps at you whenever you flirt with another man.
- You get excited by his jealousy when you flirt.
- He accuses you of wanting to sleep with other men.
- You think flirting is a harmless way to get attention.
- He thinks it is disrespectful of you to flirt with other men.
- You think he's making a big deal out of nothing.

The problem in this situation

When you bat your eyes and tilt your head when talking to another man—or type "xoxo" to your male buddies on Facebook—your partner sees a movie reel in his head of you having sex: but not with him. He can't help but connect your present flirty behavior to your sexual past. He also believes it predicts future behavior. And he's not exactly wrong: sex researcher Timothy Perper describes flirting as opening "a window of potential. Not yes, not no." It is this potential that your partner finds unbearable.

What he really means & what he really needs

When your partner asks you to stop flirting, he is asking you to choose sides—in effect, saying, "It's me or him." He feels threatened by the man with whom you are flirting and is also embarrassed by your behavior.

What you need to say and do

If your partner tells you your flirting bothers him, stop your behavior before the situation escalates. Keeping it up will only cause him to feel like you don't care about his feelings or respect his boundaries. Refocus your attention on him and reassure him he is your top priority.

- Set your Facebook status to publicly show your affection for your partner with a status message like, "...is a lucky to be with such an amazing guy!"
- Flirt with your partner by sending him text messages throughout the week.

What not to say and do

Dr. Gail Saltz, psychiatrist and frequent contributor to the *Today* show, explains that though some jealousy is normal, it will eventually destroy a relationship if not kept in check. She advises couples to work on developing a healthy relationship to avoid jealousy and its consequences. Since you know flirting causes your partner to feel jealous, avoid it.

- Never flirt with your husband or boyfriend's friends, coworkers, or family members.
- Don't tell your partner you wouldn't have to flirt if he was more fun, interesting, attractive, affluent, successful, etc.
- Never flirt with other men online.

How both of you will benefit

Hearing him out on this issue without being dismissive or defensive is an important step in the maturing of your relationship. But don't stop there—take this opportunity to quietly reflect on each of your expectations for your relationship. It will bring you closer together and serve as a welcome reminder that you are—happily and by choice—each other's number one. For as Nathaniel Hawthorne once wrote, "Happiness is a butterfly, which when pursued is always beyond your grasp, but which, if you will sit down quietly, may alight upon you."

Things to Realize
- The temporary rush flirting provides is not worth the anguish it causes your partner.
- There are many other, less hurtful ways to get attention.
- Though usually harmless, flirting can become a precursor to infidelity.

Keep Male Friends At Bay

Be wary of letting any male friend take on a role that is above or closer than your partner.

The Scenario

You have become good friends with a male co-worker. He invites you to lunch a few times a week and has suggested you have happy hour on Fridays after work. Your partner thinks this guy is out to steal you from him, and sees your interactions with him as threatening, even though you say they are harmless and friendly.

Situation at a Glance

- He is uncomfortable with your friendship with a male co-worker.
- You do not see this friendship as a threat to your marriage.
- He asks a lot of questions about what you do and talk about when you are with this male friend.
- You get defensive and flustered and become increasingly private about the friendship.

- He thinks your coworker is developing feelings for you.
- You assure him you are just friends.

The problem in this situation

When married women have close male friends, perception is everything. Your partner perceives your friendship with a male co-worker as heading toward an affair—and he's probably not the only one. It's likely your office mates have noticed your friendship and are talking about it as well. The overall perception is that something is wrong with this friendship. Thomas Bradbury, psychologist and principle investigator of the UCLA Marriage and Family Development Study, suggests that perception is often accurate: many affairs actually start with this type of friendship.

What he really means & what he really needs

Your husband fears he is losing you to your male friend—or at least part of you. He is envious of the time you spend with him and curious about what level of intimacy you share. Even if you are not having a physical affair, you may be having an emotional one, and he needs to know that neither is the case.

What you need to say and do

Stanley Charnofsky, therapist and psychology professor at Cal State Northridge, says that male friends can end up on the receiving end of "platonic perks" that are lacking in a marriage. Such perks include lively conversations and the development of an emotional connection. To preserve the sanctity of your marriage, maintain a certain distance between you and your male friends—and reserve these "perks" for your partner.

- Treat your friendships with other men as secondary to the one with your husband or boyfriend.
- Limit your interaction with male friends.
- Invite your partner to lunch or drinks with your male coworker.

What not to say and do

Your partner is not alone in being unable to accept your close friendship with another man. According to a 2008 study published in the *Los Angeles Times*, more than 25 percent of middle-aged men and 45 percent of women think it is unacceptable for married people to have friends of the opposite sex. Help your partner realize he is your number one by avoiding the following:

- Avoid accusing him of being "just jealous."

- Don't vow to never give up your guy pal.
- Never lie about time spent with a male friend.

How both of you will benefit

Many women are swept away by the excitement, attention, and novelty of having a friendship with a man who is not their husband or boyfriend. It often rekindles a fire that the doldrums of everyday life have doused. Take these emotions and fire them back toward your relationship—you will end up invigorating it and demonstrating loyalty and commitment to your best guy.

Questions to Ask Yourself

- Do I do anything special to my appearance before meeting my male friend?
- Am I completely honest with my partner about the activities and conversations we engage in?
- Is pursuing this friendship worth threatening my relationship?

Relegate Your Ex to the Past

Understand that men feel their partner's loyalty and commitment through their actions, rather than through words.

The Scenario

You frequently tell your partner that he's the only one for you, yet you still email and Facebook with an ex-boyfriend—and even get together with him now and then. Your partner is threatened by your ongoing interactions with your ex and sees you as having just one foot in the relationship.

Situation at a Glance

- You always tell your partner how devoted you are.
- He views your contact with an ex as proof that you are not rooted in your present relationship.
- You don't understand why talking to your ex once in awhile affects your current relationship.
- He often says, "Actions speak louder than words."

- You want to prove you are loyal, faithful, and committed to your partner, but aren't sure how to show him.

The problem in this situation

Though you frequently tell him you are committed, your partner is not convinced—because your actions tell him otherwise. Esteemed social psychologist Michael Argyle pointed out in his book, *The Psychology of Interpersonal Behaviour*, that nonverbal communication is necessary to establish and maintain relationships. In other words, actions and physical cues confirm or deny emotions and attitudes that are expressed verbally. This essential nonverbal component is what's missing from the way you communicate your loyalty to your partner.

What he really means & what he really needs

Telling your man he is the only one but staying in contact with your ex sends a mixed message. It says, "I love you, but I'm not over him." He needs you to make a grand gesture to back up your words, like severing ties with your ex once and for all. Unless you have children with your previous partner, this is not an unreasonable request. Staying in contact with an old boyfriend makes your current mate wonder whether you're invested in your present relationship or stuck in the past.

What you need to say and do

He needs you to demonstrate your commitment through actions, not words. Learn how to think like your mate. Start by asking him what commitment looks like to him, and then work to meet those expectations that are attainable. For example:

- Cut ties with your ex boyfriend.
- Give your current boyfriend a key to your apartment, a drawer in your dresser, or surprise him with a pair of pajamas to keep at your place.
- Prepare his favorite meal on the night of a sporting event or TV show he likes to watch and offer to watch it with him.

What not to say and do

Don't cling to an old boyfriend just to make the point that you are free to do as you wish. Terrence Real, director of the Relational Life Institute, warns couples to avoid going down a path of "losing strategies"—one of which is sticking to your guns just to be right.

- Don't talk negatively about you partner to your ex.
- Don't let pride get in the way of showing loyalty to your man.

- Stop telling your partner you are committed, and start showing him.

How both of you will benefit

Your partner will be relieved that your ex is out of the picture! As a result, he will be less tense, more trusting, and will finally believe you when you say he's "it." You will both enjoy the benefits of deepening your commitment to each other by communicating it in ways you can both understand—verbally and nonverbally.

Questions to Ask Yourself

- What do I get out of staying in touch with my ex?
- What nonverbal cues do I use to tell my partner that I love him?
- What can I do today to show my partner how much he means to me?

Stop Acting Single

Your partner is actually very insecure and needs to be reassured of your commitment and loyalty to him.

The Scenario

You go out to bars or dancing with your single girlfriends every weekend and always have a story about how many guys were hitting on your group. You think he should be happy that you are so desirable, but instead he feels resentful. Your partner feels insecure and threatened by this "single girl" behavior and wonders if you will ever settle down and act like you are in a relationship.

Situation at a Glance

- He's ready to settle down.
- You want go out with the girls and party on the weekends.
- He thinks it's time for you to grow up.
- You feel like he is trying to control you.
- He feels threatened by your single girl behavior.

- You feel stifled by his request that you go out less often, to different kinds of places, or with different people.

The problem in this situation

You and your mate are not operating in the same relationship zone. He's ready to settle down, and you want the best of both worlds—to be in a monogamous relationship yet still act like you're single.

What he really means & what he really needs

Consider what American business writer Peter F. Drucker meant when he wrote, "Unless a commitment is made there are only promises and hopes; but no plans." Your partner wants to move past the "promises and hopes" stage of your relationship and start making plans. He needs to know that you are on the same page with him, that you are ready to settle down and start building a life together—a life that does not include partying every weekend with your single friends.

What you need to say and do

You must dig deep and think about whether you are ready for what your partner is asking—for you to settle down and "grow up." If you want to stay with this man, you may have to choose an identity—loyal girlfriend or single party-girl. If you decide this relationship is right for you:

- Enroll in sexy salsa lessons with your partner so you can still get your groove on.
- Go out just one night on the weekend, and while you're out, act in a way your partner would be proud of.
- Invite your partner to go dancing with you.

What not to say and do
Your partner has made himself vulnerable to you by sharing he is uncomfortable with your single girl behavior. He has also made it clear he is ready to deepen his commitment and is asking you to do the same. His fragile ego is in your hands, so don't assert your independence by shaming, embarrassing, or being sarcastic with him on this issue.

- Don't string him along if you have no intention of settling down with him.
- Honestly assess your reasons for acting like you are still single.
- Don't invite your partner out with your friends and then ignore him all night.

How both of you will benefit

Soul searching now about your compatibility with your partner may save you both from an expensive heartache later. Indeed, with nearly 50 percent of all marriages ending in divorce, it is best to have an honest conversation about each of your expectations, values, and levels of commitment. You will likely realize you share many core values with your partner and find it easier than you thought to trade in your single girl behavior for a more mature, committed relationship. As American Mormon leader Brigham Young once wrote, "Honest hearts produce honest actions."

Questions to Ask Yourself

- Am I ready for the commitment my partner is asking me to make?
- How I can nurture my "wild side" in ways that won't contradict my loyalty to my partner?
- Am I willing to let go of my single girl behavior to save my relationship?

Tips & Exercises

Use the following activities,
tips and advice to enhance your sense
of commitment and fidelity.

Practice Making Loyalty Work for You

Your man needs to know that you are loyal, that he's the only one, and that you intend to stick around. He judges your level of commitment by matching up what you say with how you act. Here are a few ways to sincerely show him that he is your one and only:

- **Don't blab his business.**

Men are intensely private beings, and as such view typical girlfriend talk as a deep betrayal on your part. It is very likely your partner will view sharing the private details of his life, or your life together, as a violation of his trust. So keep the things he asks you to keep private to yourself, and find other fodder for girlfriend chat.

- **Make an effort to enjoy his favorites.**

Everyone feels special when the person they love notices what they like and enjoys it with them. With this in mind, buy tickets to a sporting event, grill steaks for dinner, take surfing lessons, or take him beer tasting at a local brewery—whatever it is, make the goal to show him that you pay attention to what he likes and want to do it with him.

- **Give him space to be quiet—or not.**

Men can be peculiar creatures when they get home from work. Maybe your man likes to be left alone; maybe he wants to chat about the day. Whatever his preference, indulge him in it from time to time. If he likes his space, let him enjoy being alone and quiet for a while and busy yourself with something you like to do, such as reading or going to the gym. If he likes to talk, take a break from what you're doing to go on a walk, sit on the patio, or just generally catch up with each other.

Openness & Communication

The scientific community is constantly conducting studies to understand why men and women communicate so differently. Studies range from measuring brain size to analyzing body language to examining the existence and effect of gender roles.

One particularly controversial "discovery" penned by neuropsychiatrist Louann Brizendine in her book, *The Female Brain*, claimed that women spoke 20,000 words per day, while men uttered about 7,000. The book was criticized by linguists for citing a disreputable source for this staggering statistic, and it was removed from further editions. Nonetheless, the world wanted to know: Do women really talk 3 times more than men?

Spin-off studies of Dr. Brizendine's work revealed that although women do talk more than men, they don't come close to saying 3 times as many words as their male counterparts. Still the perception of men, women, and communication is that women talk too much and men don't listen. Adding fuel to the "men don't listen" fire is a study led by Dr. Joseph T. Lurito, assistant radiology professor at Indiana University School of Medicine. Dr. Lurito measured blood flow to the brain while participants listened to a recording of John Grisham's novel, *The Partner.* Lurito announced that evidence gathered from his tests suggested that men used just half of their brain to listen, whereas women used both sides. Did this finally prove that women are better listeners than men? Not necessarily, but a media blitz ensued with headlines that announced there was finally a scientific explanation for why men don't appear to listen.

Figure out why he does what he does:

1. He avoids talking about problems because giving voice to them makes them seem worse. Besides, talking is pointless to many men—solving problems is what matters most to them.

2. He zones out when you stop talking facts and

start talking feelings or begin to gossip.

3. He doles out details sparingly because he doesn't pay attention to or care about them.

Scientists cannot prove that women talk as much as men think they do or that men are as terrible at listening as women think they are. But researchers will never run out of subject matter as long as men and women continue to perfect the art of miscommunication between the sexes. The following chapter will help you improve communication in your relationship so that even if you and your partner aren't saying the same number of words, you're both listening to what the other means.

Don't Force Him to Talk

Men think talking about problems makes them worse.

The Scenario

Your husband lost his job and you want to help him process how this affects him, both professionally and personally. You also want to discuss what it means for the family as a whole. He tells you he doesn't want to talk about it and that everything will work itself out. You are frustrated by his lack of communication and feel shut out and shut down.

Situation at a Glance

- He will only state the facts of the situation.
- You want to know the ins-and-outs of what happened and also to talk about how he feels.
- He thinks his feelings are irrelevant.
- You want to share his burden.
- He wants to be left alone to fix the problem.
- You want to be included so you can help.

The problem in this situation

You want to talk, he doesn't. Here's why: When men are forced to share their feelings on an uncomfortable topic, their bodies release the stress hormone cortisol. Increased cortisol levels have negative effects on the body, such as raising blood pressure, insulin levels, and the amount of freely circulating amino acids. Dr. Steven Stosny, co-author of *How to Improve Your Marriage Without Talking About It: Finding Love beyond Words*, notes that men are most likely to experience these negative side effects when they feel ashamed or as though they've failed.

What he really means & what he really needs

He is asking you to trust him to take care of the problem. His ego took a hit when he was laid off, and he wants to lick his wounds in private. Give him time to recover his dignity by not forcing him to talk about his feelings, since it will only make him feel worse. To restore his pride he needs to say as little as possible. Instead, he needs to focus on formulating a plan of recovery and begin executing it.

What you need to say and do

Keep an upbeat, positive attitude, and let him know you are there if he needs to talk, but don't push him to open up. Realize that your husband's self-esteem is tied to his work and in being able to provide for his family. Give him space to process his feelings on his own as he works to rebuild his confidence.

- Show him you believe in him by allowing him to handle this issue on his own.
- Tell him you are confident he will get another job, because he works hard and is a valuable employee.
- Ask to plan for a time to talk about practicalities, such as paying bills, or whether you need to pick up more hours at your job, so he does not feel ambushed or overwhelmed.

What not to say and do

As much as you want to help him, avoid thinking you can solve the problem by getting him to talk about it. Men believe that discussing problems makes them worse since talking about them only highlights their failures. Plus, not only is his pride wounded by being unemployed, he is also probably reeling from being unseated as the primary breadwinner, since 75 percent of American men fill this role.

- Don't take his mood swings personally. A *BBC News* survey revealed 1 in 5 men have aggressive outbursts as a result of work-related stress.
- Avoid discussing the details of your husband's job

loss with others—it will further embarrass him.
- Refrain from offering suggestions for how he can improve his job search.

How both of you will benefit
The Institute for Social and Economic Research at the University of Essex conducted a study that discovered when a man loses his job, there is a 33 percent increase in the odds that the couple will divorce within a year. To preserve your marriage, allow your mate space to cope in his own way. Weathering this tragedy on his terms demonstrates that you have confidence in his ability to fix things and recover.

Things to Realize
- His self-esteem suffers when he talks about losing his job.
- Men are doers, not talkers.
- He will likely return to his old self when he starts working.

Spare Him the Details

Men don't need or want to hear every little thought, just the ones that ultimately matter.

The Scenario

Your husband asks you about your day. You start to tell him about it—beginning with how your alarm didn't go off, what outfit you wore, and how long it took you to get to work. You notice his eyes glaze over and that he seems detached. You get mad, because what was the point of asking if he's clearly not going to listen?

Situation at a Glance

- He asks about your day, expecting to hear whether it was good or bad.
- You want him to feel like he was right there with you, so you give lots of details.
- He zones out after the first few sentences.
- You can tell he is not paying attention.
- He becomes restless and wants out of the conversation.

- Your feelings are hurt and you start an argument.

The problem in this situation

Your husband asks you about your day to check in with you, and to quite literally hear whether it was good or bad. Going on about every detail from the moment you awake is like drowning a man who asked for a sip of water. Milton Wright, author of the classic guide, *The Art of Conversation*, put it best when he wrote, "Discussion...must be interesting, relevant, pointed and, in general conversation, usually short."

What he really means & what he really needs

Your partner wants a succinct answer to a specific question. He does not need to hear what you told Sally over lunch or that you think you should have worn your brown shoes instead of your black ones. Though sharing these details is your way of making an intimate connection, for him, they're torture to sit through. So he zones out. To avoid flooding him with information he doesn't care to know, just answer his question and leave it at that. If he wants more information, he'll probably ask for it.

What you need to say and do

Results of a 2007 Iowa State University study confirm what many men and women have long suspected:

that women dominate the conversation at home. From your partner's perspective, you tend to dominate the conversation with details. To avoid boring him—and getting your feelings hurt when he zones out—know the difference between having a conversation with him and talking at him.

- Consider the listening threshold of your audience, and talk accordingly.
- Listen to what your partner is asking before you respond.
- Save elaborate story-telling for your girlfriends or family if your partner does not appreciate it.

What not to say and do

Try not to take it personally when your guy gets that faraway look in his eye. He simply does not have the attention span to listen to as many details as you would like to provide. Instead of starting a fight about how he never listens, change your method of delivering information.

- Don't accuse him of ignoring you, not caring, or being disinterested. It will only start a fight.
- Don't expect to have the same relationship with your husband that you have with one of your girlfriends.

- Don't become passive-aggressive or behave like a martyr.

How both of you will benefit

One of the lead researchers in the Iowa State University study, Assistant Professor of Human Development and Family Studies Megan Murphy, notes that women use talk to exert power and control in their relationships. However, when you acknowledge your partner's needs in conversation, you transform talk in your home from a dictatorship into a democracy. As a result, everyone will enjoy the conversation more.

Questions to Ask Yourself

- Does my partner's question require a lengthy response or a brief answer?
- Why do I want to shower my partner with so many details?
- Does he provide nonverbal cues that he is bored before I lose him when I talk?

Read His Non-Verbal Cues

For men, silently going about their business is not an indication that something is wrong.

The Scenario

You had a very busy day and forgot to pick up your husband's suit from the dry cleaners the day before he has an important meeting scheduled. When you tell him, he says nothing, but immediately leaves the house to go pick it up. You assume he's livid and worry a big fight is brewing for when he gets home.

Situation at a Glance

- He asked you to pick up his suit at the dry cleaners.
- You got busy and forgot.
- He doesn't say much of anything when you tell him, but rushes from the house to retrieve the suit.
- You are worried that he is mad at you.
- He just wants his suit before the dry cleaner closes.

The problem in this situation

You are probably looking at this situation from your perspective. Meaning, if the scenario was reversed and he forgot to pick up your dry cleaning, you would be angry and storm out of the house to get it. When you returned with your clothes you would let him know how disappointed you were and an argument might ensue. However, you are reading too much into your husband's response. He is operating under a completely different thought process that is fairly easy to understand.

What he really means & what he really needs

In this case your husband's silence means he is filtering out all outside input as he works to come up with a solution to his problem. Though he was probably annoyed at first, he won't hold a grudge. In fact, by the time he gets home it is likely he will forget you were supposed to pick up his suit in the first place. What he needs is for you to apologize once and then drop it.

What you need to say and do

Stephanie Booth's article, "Six Body Language Mistakes All Couples Make," in the August 2006 issue of *Cosmopolitan* warns that misinterpreting your partner's body language leads to unnecessary conflicts. To get really good at reading your partner's nonverbal communication, study his body language. Compare his posture, hand placement, facial expression, and stance when he is angry to when he is simply focused.

- Explain why you forgot, apologize once, and offer to take care if it next time.
- Ask him once if he is mad, accept his answer, and move on.
- Make the situation playful by flirting. For example, ask suggestively if there is anything you can do to make it up to him.

What not to say and do

Ignore impulses that direct you to put yourself in your husband's shoes. Otherwise, you will blow this scenario way out of proportion and cause an argument. If that happens, he really will be mad! Instead, remember Newton's Third Law: "For every action there is an equal and opposite reaction." Trying to force your partner to admit he is angry when he isn't sets him up to eventually become as mad as you feared he was over the suit.

- Don't turn a simple mistake into a full-blown issue.
- Don't berate yourself for being a terrible wife.
- Don't blame him for asking you to do the errand in the first place if you agreed to get it done.

How both of you will benefit

Though men are leaders in the outside world, they are followers in the home. This means you set the tone for what happens when a situation has the potential to turn into an argument. If you decide it is not a big deal, then chances are it won't be. Regularly apply this logic to dicey scenarios within your relationship to ease tensions and send your partner bragging to his friends about his ultra-cool, laid-back wife or girlfriend.

Questions to Ask Yourself

- Do I think my partner is angry because of something he said? Or, is it because I would be mad if the situation was reversed?
- Am I able to stay cool to keep tempers from flaring?
- How will I benefit by forcing my husband to "confess" that he is angry?

Let Go of
the Small Stuff

Sometimes he leaves out details to avoid
hurting your feelings or to prevent
causing an argument.

The Scenario
Your partner returns from an evening out with his
friends. He gives you an overview of his night but leaves
out that one of his friends brought his new girlfriend.
You find out and assume this means he lied about "no
women on guys' night." You are upset because you
wanted to go but he said you couldn't.

Situation at a Glance
- He stuck to the guys-only rule.
- You accepted it since none of the other wives or
  girlfriends were going.
- He didn't tell you his friend brought his new
  girlfriend.
- You found out from a friend and your feelings
  are hurt.

- He didn't mention it because he didn't want to upset you.
- You feel rejected and lied to.

The problem in this situation

Humorist Dave Barry once quipped, "They [men] are just what they appear to be. Tragically." Barry's statement is probably true of your guy. He did not have any mysterious motivations, nor did he leave you out of guy's night to hurt your feelings. But because you often have complex emotions and motivations, you assume there is more to his story, even when there isn't.

What he really means & what he really needs

In this case, your partner means exactly what he says. There is no subtext, nor ill intention hidden behind his words. He did not invite you to guys' night because he thought it would be "guys only." Your partner did not know his buddy was bringing a new girlfriend. He realized her presence would upset you, so he didn't mention it. Once you found out, he went into damage-control mode. What he needs is for you to let him off the hook for this one.

What you need to say and do

Columnist Joe Queenan writes in *Women's Health*

magazine, "When women refuse to let go, it's usually because the offending party—a spouse, a boyfriend—is guilty of a crime suggesting a serious flaw in moral character." Think about the circumstances of this argument and decide what makes more sense: that your husband is lacking in moral character, or that he left out a minor detail to avoid hurting your feelings?

- Explain why you are upset without assassinating your partner's character or insulting his friends.
- Trust that he had good intentions.
- Decide to believe him this time, and drop it.
- Make it clear you'd love to join him and his friends next time if women are invited.

What not to say and do

The gravity of this situation is only as heavy as you make it. Your partner made a mistake in judgment. He admitted he was wrong, explained why he did it, and then apologized. What happens next is up to you, but know that holding a grudge will weigh you down, so try to avoid it. As author Norman Vincent Peale wisely wrote in *The Power of Positive Thinking*, "Resentment or grudges do no harm to the person against whom you hold these feelings but every day and every night of your life, they are eating at you."

- Don't bring up past issues during an argument.
- Avoid using "always" and "never" when talking to him.
- Avoid harboring resentment toward your partner.
- Don't insist he stop attending guys' night as punishment.

How both of you will benefit

Your partner will appreciate that you maintained perspective and gave him the benefit of the doubt. He will also be relieved that you did not blow the situation out of proportion or punish him unfairly. As a result, he will be more inclined to share details with you the next time something doesn't go as planned.

Things to Realize

- Your partner has no reason to lie to you if you are open to hearing the truth.
- You control how serious this argument gets.
- Lugging around resentment and holding grudges prevents you from enjoying your relationship.

Tips &
Exercises

Use the following activities,
tips and advice to enhance your
openness and communication.

Getting to Know Him ... All Over Again

It is hard to imagine there is anything you don't know about your partner, but work, domestic, and social obligations have probably prevented you from keeping up on his evolving opinions, goals, values, and desires. Don't assume the person you are with today is the same person you got together with years ago. Use the following exercise to talk about the things your partner thinks and enjoys at this moment in time. You don't have to sit down and ask him these questions all at once — slip them naturally into conversation and be pleasantly surprised at his answers.

Ask him:

1. Why is (name of sports player) your favorite athlete?

2. What qualities do you admire/detest in your boss?

3. If you had your way, how often would we have sex?

4. What sexual fantasy would you like me to fulfill?

5. What's your favorite part of my body?

6. What is your ideal meal?

7. What is the funniest prank you ever pulled in college?

8. How can I make it easier for you talk about your feelings?

9. What is it about your favorite movie that allows you to watch it over and over again?

10. What hopes and dreams do you have for our children?

11. What is the best album you've heard this year?

12. If we had $5,000 to drop on a vacation, where would you want to go?

13. What is your favorite part about your job? What is your least favorite part about your job?

14. If we were to renovate part of our house, what room/area would you like to start with?

15. What is one thing you'd love to buy for yourself but worry is too expensive?

Priorities
& Values

Feminist and social justice activist Gloria Steinem once said, "Women are not going to be equal outside the home until men are equal in it." And indeed, both men and women have made great strides toward balancing the career-and-home seesaw in the last few decades.

Yet according to a 2007 poll published by the Fawcett Society, 69 percent of women still think that men need to do more housework. Women weren't the only ones who thought this—a full 56 percent of men also said their gender should probably be pitching in more when it comes to grocery shopping, doing the laundry, cleaning, and other chores. The poll results also showed that 60 percent of women and 51 percent of men believe that dads should be more involved in childcare and that women currently bear the brunt of feeding, dressing, and looking after the kids. In general, it seems as though men and women agree that men don't do enough around the house.

The reasons why men are reluctant to take on their fair share of household duties, however, are not so clear. In a *Newsweek* article titled "Men Will Be Men," writer Tony Dokoupil points out that although men have taken on more duties traditionally done by women, very little has changed to actually define manhood over the last century. Dokoupil writes that modern dads see changing diapers and other fatherhood duties as a challenge, possibly even a threat, to their identity as men, and thus struggle to find ways to express and assert themselves as "Men" rather than as simply "male." This is perhaps one explanation for why men are reluctant to roll up their sleeves and take ownership of what has for centuries been looked upon as women's work.

Figure out why he does what he does:

1. Men are creatures of habit and take longer to adjust to big life changes, such as becoming a father.

2. Men require the companionship of other men.

3. Men need to feel competent, in control of their own lives, and like they are providing for their families.

The way your guy sorts out his identity and tests his manhood may cause him to screw up now and then. As a result of his internal struggle between traditional manhood and enlightened equality-master, he is likely to get his priorities mixed up, question his values as he grows, and throw rebellious tantrums now and then.

Help Him
Become a Dad

He is less comfortable with parenthood
than you are and falls back on familiar
activities when pushed out of his comfort zone.

The Scenario
Your husband continues to be busy with sports, hobbies,
and nights out with friends even after your first baby is
born. You tell him you feel like he needs to grow up
and act like a father. He says since you leave him out of
most of the childcare duties (feeding, changing, burping,
bathing, soothing) he doesn't see a need to change his
lifestyle that much.

Situation at a Glance
- He hasn't had to sacrifice much of his personal life
  since your baby was born.
- Your life has changed a lot, and it annoys you that
  he continues living his life as he did before the baby.
- He does not feel included in childcare duties.
- You don't think he needs an invitation from you to

help care for the baby.

- He defers to you since you know what you are doing.
- You think he is capable of figuring it out if he truly wants to—after all, you did!

The problem in this situation

You are going through the very normal growing pains of new parenthood. You're just not doing it together. According to an eight-year study conducted by the University of Denver and the National Institutes of Health, you are like most new parents. The study found that 90 percent of couples experienced a decrease in marital satisfaction after their first baby was born.

What he really means & what he really needs

Men don't come to parenthood as easily as women do. In fact, according to *Men's Health* magazine, 1 in 25 suffer from postnatal depression (PND) after the birth of their first child. A man's mood plummets due to changes in his lifestyle and in the relationship. He needs you to bring him into the parenting experience and show him around. Though you're new mom, you seem confident, and he could use your guidance.

What you need to say and do

Invite your husband to participate in the activities and rituals you do with your child. Ask him to sit with you while you feed the baby, or let him bottle feed the baby each day. As much as moms don't like to admit it, they tend to hijack the baby's first year. Encourage him when he does participate and leave him in charge of baby's care part of each day to build confidence.

- Help him adapt to fatherhood by trusting him to care for the baby by himself.
- Tell him you understand how he feels, because you feel the same way!
- Let him learn by doing.

What not to say and do

Instead of resenting your husband, tell him you need him home more often. And don't assume that because he is out that he doesn't value time spent with you and baby. It's more likely that you are his top priority, but he just doesn't know how to properly express it.

- Don't forget that men do what's comfortable when faced with unknowns. He continues to do what is familiar because he is insecure in his role as father.
- Don't criticize him when he puts the diaper on wrong or forgets to warm the bottle.

- Don't tell him you don't need him. It will cause him to retreat further away from the family.
- Don't get frustrated and do things for him. The only way he will learn is if he makes mistakes and does it himself.

How both of you will benefit

Though women will probably always bear the bulk of family duties, men are getting better at making their families a top priority. Couples that work as a team, share the same values, and make time for each other will find themselves among the 10 percent that report an increase in marital satisfaction after having children.

Questions to Ask Your Partner

- How can I help you feel more comfortable taking care of our child?
- Do I ever discourage you from embracing fatherhood?
- What changes can you make for the good of our family?

Compromise
On His Friends

You can set limits and still encourage your
partner's need for male camaraderie.

The Scenario

You are sick of your partner's friends coming over
several nights a week. When they are over, they drink a
lot of beer, eat a lot of food, talk loudly and curse, and
leave a huge mess. When you ask him to stop having
them over to the house, he gets angry and you end up in
a huge fight.

Situation at a Glance

- He enjoys having his friends over for drinks, to
  watch the game, or just to hang out.
- You think they are over too often.
- He thinks it's good for the kids to be exposed
  to adults.
- You think it's inappropriate to drink so much in
  front of children.

- He wants you to lighten up. He's just having fun.
- You have considered yelling at him in front of his friends so they are too embarrassed to come back.

The problem in this situation

Your partner is torn between two worlds and is trying to fuse them together. He wants to be home with his family, but also out socializing with his friends—so he does it at home. You view his behavior as childish and insensitive to your vision of what home life should be. There is a way to compromise, but neither of you can see it because you are on the offensive and he is postured to defend himself.

What he really means & what he really needs

Sociologist Michael Kimmel, author of *Guyland*, put it best when he explained that a guy's task is to "navigate the passage from adolescence to adulthood without succumbing to the most soul-numbing, spirit-crushing elements that surround him every day." Your partner's behavior is his way of counter-balancing the "spirit-crushing elements" of his daily life.

What you need to say and do

Just as you need your girlfriends, so too does your partner need his guy friends. Still, it is possible to work together to establish boundaries and set limits without emasculating him.

- Think of how miserable he would become (and make you) if you forbid him from spending time with his friends!
- Come to a compromise on how often they can come over, what time they must leave, and how much they will drink in front of your kids.
- Get in girl time so you do not resent guys' night.

What not to say and do

Avoid dropping passive-aggressive comments like, "I was going to make dinner tonight, but your friends kept me up until 4 a.m. and I need a nap instead." If the guys were too loud, just come out and say it. Though you are frustrated, don't resort to insults or public humiliation to force your guy to change.

- Don't cut your partner down in public or in private.
- Avoid asking him to sacrifice his friendships for family.
- Don't withhold sex as punishment for his time spent with friends.
- Never force him to choose between you and his friends.

How both of you will benefit

Working out kinks in a relationship is not always easy, but it is possible if both partners make compromises instead of trying to change one another. As Danish philosopher Søren Kierkegaard wisely wrote, "Love does not alter the beloved, it alters itself." Deepen your respect for one another by appreciating each other as individuals. At the same time, cultivating tolerance and consideration for the other person's needs and values will reduce resentment, tension, and other negative feelings that arise when people try to control each other.

Checklist for Action

- Ask your partner to have friends over just a couple nights a month, and be nice to them when they are there.
- Tell him in private that it bothers you that he drinks in front of the kids.
- Don't purposely plan family events on guys' night.
- Establish personal boundaries without becoming overly controlling.

Honor His Experiences

Men often have strong opinions about their own upbringing and either want to mimic or avoid parallels in their own families.

The Scenario

Your husband wants to send the children to private school because he went to one and values the experience. You would prefer to save money and send the kids to the local public school which has a great reputation, but you can't convince him this is an acceptable option.

Situation at a Glance

- He wants the kids to attend an expensive private school.
- You think public school is fine and you'd rather save the money for your child's college tuition.
- He attributes his success to his private school education.
- You are insulted because you went to public school.
- He believes a private education instills values that public education does not.

- You think he is acting like a snob.

The problem in this situation

You are both so focused on the details that you can't see the big picture. You and your husband agree that you want the best for your child's education, just not on the means for getting there. This argument is not unique to your relationship, as everyone from private citizens to government officials debates the value of private versus public education. The problem is that you are each taking the discussion personally—an argument against public schools is an attack against you, and vice versa.

What he really means & what he really needs

Men view it as their duty to pass on their knowledge, experience, and successes to their children. The components of his childhood that he cherishes—such as religious teachings, values, work ethic, and education—are part of this legacy. Therefore, it does not seem outrageous to him that the National Association of Independent Schools reports that the median tuition in 2005-2006 for grades 1 through 3 at private schools was $14,000. Rather, it is a matter of pride to pay a premium to give this part of his upbringing to his own children.

What you need to say and do

Think about the elements of your own childhood that you feel strongly about sharing with your children. Also, consider the parts you would never pass down to them. Once you have a grasp on your own convictions, tell your husband that you understand his position. Be open to discussing several options and present your own research on the public school system in your area to show him you take this matter seriously.

- Genuinely consider the pros and cons of both sides.
- Ask him to state his view without insults or name-calling.
- Schedule appointments to visit both kinds of schools.

What not to say and do

Whatever you ask of your husband—patience, calm, to respectfully hear you out—you must also give. Don't expect your partner to respect your ideas and then attack his.

- Don't cling to your point of view so tightly that you cannot see your husband's.
- Don't attack his character with comments such as, "Private school is what turned you into such a control freak!"

- Don't give up your convictions just to end an argument, or you will end up resenting the decision and your husband.

How both of you will benefit
Create ground rules for how to talk about heated issues such as your opposing views on educational values before having the actual discussion. It is akin to laying out the lesson plan before getting up in front of the class. Establishing rules of engagement creates limits for what is considered "fair game" and limits the potential for a discussion to turn into a war. It's okay to argue. Just keep your verbal punches above the belt line.

Questions to Ask Your Partner
- How do you imagine we'll pay for private school and college? Can you draft up a plan?
- Would you consider sending the kids to private elementary school and then to public high school?
- Do you understand why I take it personally when you attack public schooling?

Practice Non-Comparison

Avoid comparing your home life and status to other couples'. And make it clear that you value his opinion above all others.

The Scenario

You frequently tell your partner what a great relationship your friend and her husband have, and you share her opinion for how to improve your relationship. Your partner seems irritable whenever you bring the subject up and you do not understand why.

Situation at a Glance

- He gets moody when you talk about your friend's fantastic relationship.
- You want to benefit from what she's told you.
- He thinks it's obnoxious that she talks about their private affairs and fears it means you do the same.
- You think he is missing the point.
- He thinks you don't value his opinion.
- You want to find a way around his ego so he doesn't miss out on some great advice.

The problem in this situation

You are honest in your admiration for your friend's relationship and your desire to learn from her. The problem is that your presentation of the other couple as "better" has triggered your guy's insecurities and makes him feel inferior. Dr. Marilyn J. Sorensen, author of *Breaking the Chain of Low Self-Esteem*, notes that once a person develops insecurities about a particular issue, it is difficult to change their perception.

What he really means & what he really needs

When you bring up your friend's marriage, your partner hears that he is a failure. He is ashamed that you hold the other couple in such high esteem and thinks you are unhappy. Dr. Aaron Kipnis, author of *Angry Young Men: How Parents, Teachers and Counselors Can Help Bad Boys Become Good Men*, writes that a man's entire sense of self becomes eroded when he experiences shame. Your partner needs you to stop comparing your relationship to the other couple and to talk with him, not your friend, about how to improve your relationship.

What you need to say and do

Change tactics and reevaluate your priorities, because as actor Harry Lloyd once said, "Success is only another form of failure if we forget what our priorities should be."

Ask yourself what matters more: forcing your partner to adopt your friend's relationship style or working together with him to improve your own relationship?

- Make suggestions for how to improve your relationship without attaching them to other "more successful" relationships.
- Tell your partner that you value his input above all others.
- Email him a "Top Ten Things That I Love About Us" list.

What not to say and do
Stop thinking that your relationship is not as good as others. This mentality is not productive and reveals that you seek solutions from outside, rather than from within. Remember that all couples have their issues, so avoid romanticizing others. If you can't help but daydream of the perfect relationship, imagine your own marriage at its height of perfection and make it a priority to strive for that image.

- Stop comparing your marriage to your friends' relationships.

- Don't point out how loving, thoughtful, smart, attractive, religious, faithful, successful, or sexy your friend's husband is.
- Avoid belittling your partner or devaluing the contributions he makes to your relationship.

How both of you will benefit

When you and your partner are on the same side, you develop an immunity to outside comparisons. You also nurture confidence in your ability to solve problems as a team. When you believe in your relationship despite its flaws, you wholeheartedly accept it. This leads to the reality that your marriage is the one to envy.

Things to Realize

- No matter how well-intended, comparisons hurt.
- Ignore outside influences and evaluate the core values you share with your partner.
- There is no such thing as a perfect relationship.

Tips &
Exercises

Use the following activities,
tips and advice to enhance your
understanding of priorities and values.

Thirty Ways to Let Him Know He's Your Top Priority

A man needs reassurance from his partner that she still values, respects, loves, and is attracted to him. Compliments serve as validation that you still notice him no matter how long you've been together. Email, text, Facebook, or simply pay verbal compliments often, and be genuine in their delivery.

Tell him...
1. I love tracing the contours of your muscles with my hands.
2. You have great hair!
3. I love looking at you.
4. You have the best smile.

5. The little wrinkles next to your eyes make me smile.

6. I want to bite your lips!

7. You make me feel safe.

8. You make me feel so loved.

9. I love how you take care of me.

10. You are a great father.

11. You are a thoughtful husband.

12. You are a true partner.

13. You make me feel like a queen.

14. You are so intuitive!

15. You are the true definition of what it means to be a man.

16. I can't imagine my life without you.

17. You are the greatest lover I've ever had.

18. Your touch lingers on my skin for days.

19. I fantasize about the way you make love.

20. Your smell drives me wild!

21. You are the only man for me.

22. You have the most capable hands.

23. I am so impressed with your reasoning skills.

24. You're right!

25. I admire your work ethic.

26. I respect you more than anyone else I know.

27. You are a good man.

28. I am proud to be your wife.

29. Marrying you was the best decision of my life.

30. You are my best friend.

Money & Finances

The recession of 2008 placed a strangle-hold around American workers' sense of job security as layoffs continued month after month.

Indeed, as 2009 kicked off, the outlook was bleak: *Forbes* magazine tracked more than a half-million layoffs by 500 of America's largest public companies between November 2008 and May 2009. The U.S. Department of Labor reports the unemployment rate jumped from 5.1 percent in March 20008 to more than 9 percent in 2009. Though most major news outlets are reporting as of summer 2009 that the recession may be easing up, the extent of the fallout, and even the true causes of the recession, have yet to be fully understood.

One thing that seems immediately clear, however, is that American men are bearing the brunt of the devastating effects of financial ruin. Because men continue to be the primary jobholders and breadwinners in the majority of families, theirs are the jobs that are being lost. Furthermore, men tend to hold many of the jobs that were being shed at a fantastic rate, such as those in the automotive and financial sectors. It is no surprise, then, that the *Financial Times* reports that 80 percent of the more than 5.1 million jobs lost since the crisis began were held by men.

The National Business Review warns that any economic decline is damaging to men not only because of the lost wages and earnings, but because it threatens both their mental health and their sense of manhood. As these qualities suffer, so too does a man's self-esteem. In some extreme cases, men are even driven to suicide, because their sense of failure is so great, they are unable to see the potential for economic or emotional recovery.

Figure out why he does what he does:

1. His identity is deeply enmeshed with his ability to work, earn, and provide.

2. Purchasing expensive gadgets is an outward sign that he is successful and accomplished.

3. He derives great pride in being the primary breadwinner.

The future is not all doom and gloom, however. With love, support, and excellent communication in his relationship, the American male will find his way back to work, recover his pride and reputation, and go on to prosper once again. For as Scottish writer Allan K. Chalmers once wrote, "The Grand essentials of happiness are: something to do, something to love, and something to hope for."

Talking about money with your partner is one of the most difficult conversations you are likely to have with him. In fact, Karen Peterson, a columnist for *USA Today*, has classified money talk as "the subject from hell." It will take patience and perseverance, but you and your mate are very capable of learning the skills required to talk about finances with as much comfort as you do any other topic.

He Needs
to be Needed

Men become emotionally distant
when they blame themselves for their
family's financial struggles.

The Scenario
The bills are piling up and it is becoming more difficult
to meet your family's monthly financial obligations. You
want to discuss solutions, but your partner shuts down
or gets angry with himself whenever you bring up your
mounting debt. You find his behavior counterproductive
and wish he'd be open to talking about the problem and
finding solutions.

Situation at a Glance
- He has trouble discussing financial issues.
- You want to improve your family's finances.
- He thinks having money problems signifies failure.
- You are frustrated with his reluctance to talk
  about money.
- He takes the details of your financial situation
  personally.

- You have no idea how to get him to cooperate.

The problem in this situation

A man's self-worth is tied up in the financial stability of his family. When there is a problem making ends meet, he feels responsible. Though you don't blame him, he does. Navigating his emotional shut-down is frustrating for you, because you want to work together to find realistic solutions. Also, you view his reaction as self-pitying and unproductive.

What he really means & what he really needs

The 2009 Pan-European Relationship Survey found that 83 percent of women prefer financial equality in their relationship; yet the majority of men continue to feel responsible for their family's financial well-being. When your partner becomes quiet, moody, or expresses self-loathing during financial discussions, he is attempting to avoid what he views as a shameful subject, one at which he has failed. With this in mind, he needs to be reassured that he is a good provider—and also made to see that dealing with your financial situation requires teamwork.

What you need to say and do

Develop a strategy for talking to your partner about finances. This might include planning your discussion ahead of time; anticipating topics on which he is likely to clam up; and being prepared with statements, bills, and budgets you've figured out in advance. Think of your overall approach as a series of diplomatic efforts instead of as a one-time bombardment.

- Schedule a family financial meeting in his Outlook or Google calendar. This gives him time to adjust to the idea and prepare.
- Stick to facts, figures, and solutions, such as, "We owe $500 in medical bills. We can pay it off in five installments of $100 each, or we can use money from our restaurant budget and pay it off sooner. Which do you prefer?"
- Point out what's going right: "We've gotten really good at sticking to our grocery budget."
- Have a positive attitude: "I know we can work together to improve our financial situation. We've already eaten away at about $2,000 of our credit card debt so far this year."

What not to say and do
Avoid triggers that cause him to get angry, distant, or feel ashamed. These include anything that can be interpreted as blaming, accusatory, or disrespectful. Establishing ground rules beforehand will help. For example:

- Avoid "you" statements during the discussion.
- Don't ever say, "This is all your fault!"
- Don't freak out. If he thinks you're panicking, he will feel like it's his fault and shut down or explode with anger.
- Avoid attacking his manhood with statements like, "Stop being such a baby and talk to me!"
- Don't take your financial issues outside of your marriage without your partner's consent.

How both of you will benefit

Learning to talk to your husband about financial concerns requires you to work together to come up with workable solutions instead of focusing on who is at fault. You can use these skills in all other areas of your marriage, too.

Things to Realize

- Even if he deals primarily with money the family's financial problems are not solely his fault.
- It requires patience to talk about money.
- Your goal is to form an alliance with your husband on money matters.

Make Him
Feel Secure

Some men are threatened when their partner
earns more money, believing it undermines
their role as primary breadwinner.

The Scenario
After receiving a long-awaited promotion, your income
is more than your partner's. Instead of being happy for
you, your partner sulks and gets quiet when you share
the good news. You are disappointed and confused by his
reaction, since you will both benefit from the money.

Situation at a Glance
- He is not enthusiastic about your income boost.
- You are hurt by his reaction.
- He feels threatened by your raise.
- You see it as money for both of you.
- He feels emasculated by your success.
- You work hard and want him to be proud of you.

The problem in this situation

Though the 2009 Pan-European Relationship Survey found that just 20 percent of women expect their partner to earn more then they do, the majority of men still prefer to be, and even are, the breadwinner. As such, men place high value their role as provider because it is integral to their overall sense of manhood. Thus, he may view the fact that you earn more than him as emasculating. You, on the other hand, see it as reward for your hard work and an opportunity to contribute to your family's financial security.

What he really means & what he really needs

Give him time to adjust to your news. Brendan Burchell from the University of Cambridge's sociology department notes that being the breadwinner is one of the few positive ways in which men are able to define themselves. Your husband needs to work out his emotions in his head, and if you force him to react before he is ready, he may say something you will both regret.

What you need to say and do

Celebrate your success and be confident you have earned it. Behaving as though you have something to apologize for only adds to his feeling that something is "wrong." Normalize the situation by believing—and acting—like you deserved a raise. Also, frame your new salary as a "win" for the entire family. For as Walt Whitman wisely wrote, "What I assume you shall assume / For every atom belonging to me as good belongs to you."

- Give him time to adjust to the new financial dynamic. He will appreciate the space to sort out his feelings.
- Let him see for himself the benefits of the extra income. For example, use your first fat paycheck to pay off a debt that has had you both stressed out for a while.
- Consider that you might be jealous of your husband if he had achieved such success at his job.
- Celebrate with friends who are not threatened by your success.

What not to say and do
Many women try to ease an uncomfortable situation by belittling their joy and accomplishments. For example, you may be tempted to tell your husband he works harder than you and that he is the one that deserves a raise, or play the whole thing off as no big deal. But nothing will soothe your husband's reaction to your earnings except time, patience, and the respectful handling of his issues.

- Don't downplay your success for his benefit. Doing so will feed his insecurity by making him feel like you pity him.
- Don't "buy" his support with lavish gifts. This will only make him feel worse.
- Don't tell family, friends, or coworkers that your husband is struggling with your raise. It will embarrass him.

How both of you will benefit

When one partner steps out of his or her role, it can throw off the status quo of the relationship, which many people find scary. But challenging yourselves to accept one another in new ways keeps your relationship fresh, exciting, and honest.

Questions to Ask Yourself
- Why do I need my partner's validation?
- Is my partner happy for me when I share good news?
- Are my expectations for his reaction realistic?

Boys Need Their Toys

Men tend to spend large sums of money on high-tech gadgets to assert their independence or status.

The Scenario

Your partner just spent several thousand dollars on a new computer and he is already talking about the "next generation" in software. You don't understand why he can't just be satisfied with the purchase as it is, or why he's always looking ahead to buy the next new gadget. You also resent his big ticket purchases since you rarely buy anything expensive for yourself.

Situation at a Glance

- He follows developments in the tech industry and creates wish lists for what to buy next.
- You are annoyed by his inability to enjoy what he has.
- He is excited by new gadgets.
- You think he wastes money on expensive electronics that will be outdated within a year.

- He takes pride in researching and building various state-of-the art electronic "systems."
- You can think of a million more practical ways to spend money.

The problem in this situation
You value practical spending on clothes, food, and home repairs, whereas he places value on keeping up with technology. You think his dedication to acquiring the latest gadgets is a waste of time and money; he thinks such purchases are more valuable than expensive dinners and drinks, because at least what he buys is tangible. In short, you and your partner have different definitions of money well-spent.

What he really means & what he really needs
Very simply, your partner wants to buy fun stuff with his hard-earned money. In many ways, he is living out his childhood dream of being able to have every brand-new, shiny toy he has ever wanted.

What you need to say and do
There are worse ways your husband could spend his money—gambling, for example. So, try to go with the flow on this one. As long as he's not breaking the family bank to keep up with the latest trend, let him be. If

he is outspending, it is likely he's going to need some evidence to persuade him to change his ways. For six months, keep track of all his extracurricular purchases (and keep track of yours). At the end of the six months, show him the bill. Seeing that he spent $3,686 on new tools, software, and a Blu-ray‾ player, while you only spent $464 on new shoes and a purse, is likely to make him realize the situation has gotten out of hand.

- Agree on an amount he can spend monthly on new toys.
- Understand that he views owning products like the iPhone as an important status symbol.
- Ask that he limit his acquisitions to things that will at least benefit you both, like a new home stereo system other than one that goes in his personal car.

What not to say and do

If you want to discourage your partner's penchant for gadgets, don't try to limit or forbid it. Doing so will have the opposite effect, as Mark Twain noted when he wrote, "The more things are forbidden, the more popular they become." Besides, nagging your husband to change what he likes mimics a parent-child relationship instead of an adult partnership, which is demeaning to you both.

- Don't ask him to completely stop buying new gadgets.
- Don't go out and buy expensive things for yourself just to show him how frustrating it is.
- Don't let him talk you into agreeing to purchases just so you can look supportive or easygoing.

How both of you will benefit

Treating each other's likes, dislikes, and hobbies with respect is necessary for preserving independence in a relationship. Think of how boring your marriage would be if you enjoyed all the same hobbies and agreed on everything! As French philosopher Voltaire wisely wrote, "All kinds are good except the kind that bores you."

Things to Realize

- You can benefit from your man's tech purchases. Camera phones, GPS, and hi-def TVs can be fun for everyone.

Be Open to Changing Roles

Men are often content to remain
detached from the household economy—
until there is a problem.

The Scenario

You handle the household finances—from paying the
mortgage and credit card bills to tracking the monthly
budget and doling out spending money. You don't mind
doing it, but it leaves you vulnerable to his criticism and
blame when there are accounting and budget issues. You
think if you are going to do all the work, he has no right
to criticize you.

Situation at a Glance

- He is hands-off when it comes to household finances.
- You have developed an efficient system for
  managing them.
- He has no idea how you run the household economy.
- You prefer for him to stay out of it.
- He doesn't seem to appreciate your hard work but is

quick to criticize when there is a problem or
mistake, such as a late payment.

- You resent his criticism and think he should either
  fully participate or keep his comments to himself.

The problem in this situation
As long as everything goes right with the household
finances, your money management skills are not called
into question. But they do seem up for debate any
time something goes wrong. He thinks he is helping
you "perfect" your system by offering feedback and
suggestions, whereas you feel unjustly criticized.

What he really means & what he really needs
Even though you, the family bookkeeper, feel as though
you inherited a thankless job that comes with little
praise or appreciation, your partner actually feels out
of the loop. His way of "plugging in" is to review your
system and make suggestions for how to improve it. He
does this to connect to the family budget and because he
feels compelled to solve problems—not to find mistakes
or harp on your accounting skills.

What you need to say and do
Offer to let your husband take over the budget to better
understand how it feels to be on the other side of the
checkbook. In fact, the makers of the online budgeting

software Quicken suggest that couples take turns managing household finances to gain an appreciation for the other's perspective. It is likely that you both will gladly return to your previous roles the very next month!

- Switch roles for one month. Expect to have bills go unpaid and accumulate late fees—these may be worth it if they prove the point that managing money takes attention.
- Opt to have credit card statements emailed to you, and then forward them to your husband so he is in the loop.
- Make your partner aware of the work it takes to manage the household economy by emailing him when you pay a bill, make a purchase, track a receipt, find a bargain, etc. He will likely be bowled over when he realizes the amount of work you put into your family's budget (and ask that you stop filling his inbox!)

What not to say and do
Try not to think your husband is personally attacking you when he suggests ways to improve the home budget. Rather, take it as a genuine, though awkward attempt to help out. Don't get defensive or angry, because this will only lead to arguments and an eventual stand-off. Your

goal is to facilitate cooperation and inclusion without sacrificing a management style that works.

- Don't be stubborn. Listen to your partner's feedback and incorporate it when he is right.
- Don't allow him to talk down to you, insult you, or make you feel like you're doing an inferior job.
- Never hide facts, cover up mistakes, or lie to your partner about the state of your family's finances.

How both of you will benefit

Being open to one another's perspective and feedback is good for your marriage. Should you feel resistant to your partner's suggestions, remember what Friedrich Nietzsche's observed: "You have your way. I have my way. As for the right way, the correct way, and the only way, it does not exist."

Checklist for Action

- Create a transparent accounting system.
- Give your partner a list of log-in names, passwords, and account numbers so he has no excuses for not participating.

Tips & Exercises

Use the following activities, tips and advice to enhance your discussion of money and finances.

Money Matters

MarriageEquality.org reports that 43 percent of couples cite finances as the primary reason they fight. While some amount of conflict over money is to be expected, unchecked hostility over your partner's economic philosophy may lead you straight to divorce court. To prevent that, work with your partner to establish some financial ground rules.

Examples include:
- Make a household budget and agree to stick to it.
  - Collect all receipts and track purchases to see where spending is in check and where it is out of control.

- Make exceptions for special expenses that are important to your partner, and he will do the same for you.

- Schedule monthly meetings to discuss financial concerns.
  - Meet two weeks before most bills are due to decrease last-minute tension.
  - Set time limits for financial discussions and agree to stop talking money when you reach it.
  - Never discuss financial matters in the bedroom.
  - Hold all of your questions/concerns/feedback for the meeting so as not to seem like you are constantly picking on your partner.

- Set financial goals as a team and agree on a plan to reach them.
  - Calculate your combined income and agree on a percentage to use for investing, a percentage for savings, and a percentage to donate to charity.
  - Include "free" money for each of you to spend with no questions asked.
  - Throw all spare change into a piggy bank for your children.

Sex &
Intimacy

On March 17, 2008, New York Governor Eliot Spitzer resigned from his post in the midst of a highly publicized scandal. Spitzer stepped down after it was revealed he had spent thousands of dollars on high-priced call girls.

Not long after Spitzer's shameful resignation, in August of that same year, potential presidential candidate John Edwards issued a statement admitting he'd had an affair with a former campaign worker after a series of allegations about their relationship ran in *The National Enquirer*.

Spitzer and Edwards are just two of more than 50 million men in the U.S. that cheat on their wives. Most of these men do not end up in the newspaper, and their wives do not get to process their feelings on *Oprah*. Indeed, for most couples, affairs are private, dirty little secrets that threaten to destroy their families and permanently ruin their self-esteem.

It's no secret that men cheat. But why men cheat still remains a mystery to the average woman. Most women assume their adulterous husbands are after "new" sex. However, a recent study conducted by marriage counselor M. Gary Neuman for his book, *The Truth About Cheating*, found that 92 percent of men cheat because they do not feel appreciated by their wives. These men initially form an emotional connection with another woman that eventually leads to sex—not the other way around. The evidence, it seems, suggests that sex is not the primary motivator of infidelity that most women believe it to be.

Of course, many relationships will not be threatened by cheating. But it is likely that at some point, you and your partner will have very different sexual needs and interests.

Figure out why he does what he does:

1. He is hardwired to have sex—and lots of it.
2. He craves spontaneity and variety.

3. Regular, satisfying sex affirms his status as a man.

Academics, therapists, sex experts, sociologists, and behavioral health professionals are beginning to acknowledge that men, like women, crave more than just the physical satisfaction of sex. When men feel unappreciated, taken for granted, rejected, or as though their partner has given up on their sex life, they may become at risk to cheat.

However, men that report feeling "highly satisfied" in their relationships are unlikely to have affairs because their emotional needs are met by their partners. And couples who agree their marriage is "above average" tend to have excellent communication skills as well as a great sex life.

Open Yourself to Intimacy

He takes it personally when you say no to sex.

The Scenario
Your partner tries to seduce you several times a week. Three out of 4 times you are too tired—or simply not in the mood—for sex, so you say, "Not now." Your partner thinks you have lost your attraction to him and gets pouty, angry, or sullen. But the reality is that you're tired, want some time to yourself, and don't want sex to turn into yet another routine obligation in your life.

Situation at a Glance
- He would have sex with you 7 days a week.
- You are content to have sex 7 times a month.
- He becomes moody and distant during dry spells.
- You feel connected by talking rather by having sex.
- He thinks you are not attracted to him.
- You are exhausted by your daily life and rarely feel sexy.

The problem in this situation

A 2002 study conducted by the National Opinion Research Center at the University of Chicago found that married couples have sex 68.5 times a year. Another study conducted in 2004 by CBS News showed that 45 percent of married couples have sex just 1 to 3 times per month. Though the numbers are daunting, the reality is that all couples experience peaks and valleys in their sex lives.

What he really means & what he really needs

When your husband wants to have sex with you, he is sending several messages at once. He wants to communicate his feelings for you in a physical way; he is turned on and wants to see it through to orgasm; and he is feeling playful, serious, romantic, lovey-dovey, or just plain frisky. Regardless of motivation, his attempt to seduce you makes him vulnerable to rejection. Say "no" too many times and you run the risk of alienating him or causing him to give up completely.

What you need to say and do

Think of having a great sex life as the foundation for building a deeply satisfying, long-lasting connection with your partner. This connection will outlast the job that makes you so tired, the errands that fatigue you, the clothes that currently make you feel unsexy, and even the small children that will someday be grown and out of the house. Without forcing yourself to physically connect, make an effort to think about how important—even sacred—intimacy with your partner truly is.

- Carve out 15 minutes of alone time each day for quiet time or meditation. This will help you feel less desperate for rest when your partner wants sex
- Get a bikini wax. You will be amazed at how sexy this new style will make you feel, and your partner will love it.
- When you feel even a little aroused, act on your impulse—don't talk yourself out of intimacy with reminders about how much you have to do or why you'd rather go to sleep.

What not to say and do

Though you should never go through the motions of having sex with your partner, there is something to be said for "letting the car warm up as you drive." In other words, let your partner persuade you to have sex even when you are not in the mood. Not every single time, but at least 50 percent of the time. More often than not you'll be glad you did and enjoy the experience.

- Don't ignore his advances. Getting no reaction is more devastating than hearing, "No," for most men.

- Don't say, "Fine, let's just get it over with!" You will kill the mood and hurt his feelings.
- Don't think your sex life will improve on its own or that your libido will return to normal "eventually." The only way to improve your sex life is to start having sex.

How both of you will benefit

Remember how you couldn't keep your hands off each other when you first met? Change how lovemaking happens in your relationship, and you will find yourself looking forward to sex and intimacy again. For example, if your guy always initiates sex, switch roles. Make love in the kitchen or the shower—somewhere out of the ordinary. Being open to seduction—and to seducing—will restore a fresh, exciting dynamic to your sex life that you will both benefit from.

Things to Realize

- This is your sex life too, and you want it to be incredible.
- You have control over your reaction to your partner.
- Initiate sex when you are in the mood.

Stop Faking It

He would never fake an orgasm,
so it doesn't occur to him that you would.

The Scenario
Your partner seems to get bored or impatient if you take a long time to reach orgasm. This stresses you out, makes you feel self-conscious, and often causes it to end up taking even longer. To avoid embarrassing yourself and hurting his feelings, you frequently pretend to climax. Although you know he can't tell the difference, you secretly resent him for not caring whether you have a real orgasm or not.

Situation at a Glance
- He is oblivious that you sometimes fake orgasms.
- You fake when you think he's bored waiting for you.
- He thinks everything is normal with your sex life.
- You think he doesn't pay close enough attention.
- He has no idea you are upset with him.
- You think he is a selfish lover.

The problem in this situation

A 2009 Sun Media/Leger Marketing poll reported in the Toronto Sun found that 49 percent of Canadian women have faked at least one orgasm. Statistics in the U.S. range from 40 to 72 percent, depending on the reporting agency. Nonetheless, even the lowest estimates reveal that close to half of all women have faked it. In the article, "Too Nice to Orgasm," sex therapist Cheryl Swan argues that each woman is responsible for her own orgasm. Relying on your partner to figure out how to bring you to orgasm puts too much pressure on him. Besides, as Swan points out, "only you know what feels good."

What he really means & what he really needs

He might become a little bored if you take a long time to reach orgasm (like you haven't ever been bored during sex!), or he may be concentrating on perfecting his technique. Either way, it's not the end of the world. If he is bored, you're not doing enough to keep him interested. Move around, moan, switch positions, or pleasure him for awhile instead.

What you need to say and do

Let go of the idea that because he can't tell whether your orgasm was real or fake that he is a self-involved lover.

In fact, you are the fraud here. Tell him he seems bored or distracted when you take awhile to climax. Let him know you care enough to keep him aroused, and then give him tips for how to bring you to orgasm. It is very likely that your partner wants to know how to make you wild with pleasure.

- Tell him when what he is doing is not working.
- Be specific when guiding him to your sweet spot. For example, tell him whether you are in the mood for oral, penile, or finger pleasure.
- Allow yourself the enjoyment of having a real orgasm.
- Practice makes perfect! Masturbate to get at the helm of your own climax controls.

What not to say and do
On average, it takes a woman's body 15 to 20 minutes to be ready for sex. In that time blood rushes to the clitoris and causes it to become sensitive and erect. From that point on is when your journey to orgasm begins. Don't shut down the process before you have a chance to climax. Instead, get in tune with your body rhythm, then teach your partner to do what works and to avoid what doesn't.

- Never tell him you faked your orgasm! He will be insulted and confused by this.
- Don't fake any more orgasms. Use the fact that you didn't climax to start a discussion about what he can do to make you feel good.
- Don't be afraid to ruin the mood. He would much rather switch to something you actually enjoy.
- Don't make coming the goal of having sex. Doing so puts too much pressure on both partners.

How both of you will benefit
Removing dishonesty from the bedroom encourages mutual enjoyment of sex. Taking the reigns on your orgasms allows you and your spouse to share an honest erotic experience.

Things to Realize
- You are responsible for your own orgasm.
- You would be hurt if you knew your spouse faked.
- Your sex life is only as good as the effort you put into it.

Take Charge in the Bedroom

He loves it when you take initiative and surprise him in the bedroom.

The Scenario

On a whim you pick up a few sex toys and a dirty movie, and introduce them to the bedroom the next time you are intimate with your partner. Your husband is thrilled and you have the best sex of your life. You are surprised by how strongly he reacted to this and want to understand what you did to elicit this response. You are also now suspicious if it was you or the toys and movie that elicited this reaction.

Situation at a Glance

- He was very excited that you thought to try new stuff.
- You felt powerful and in control.
- He got off on your take-charge attitude.
- You felt empowered by the whole experience.
- He can't stop talking about how great the sex was.

- You agree, but now wonder if it was you or the stuff that made it so great.

The problem in this situation

A 2006 *Elle*/MSNBC.com Sex and Love Survey discovered that just 49 percent of men are "satisfied" or "very satisfied" with their sex lives. A full 24 percent of men even reported that they are "very dissatisfied." The unhappiest respondents say they are often bored in the bedroom. So purchasing toys and introducing them as a surprise was a brave, bold move, and the exact quality men crave in a sexual partner. The only problem is that now that you've shown you can think outside the box, he will expect you to do it more often!

What he really means & what he really needs

His excitement over the toys and movie is truly about you. Taking the initiative to try something new told your mate you think about having sex with him even when you're apart. He finds this incredibly hot. To encourage you to keep it up, he will tell you over and over just how hot he thought it was. For him this is a turning point in his sex life—a moment that proves that chemistry and heat are not a thing of the past. He needs you to nurture this new and innovative version of your sex life.

What you need to say and do

You already have positive feedback from your partner. Your experiment worked, and it is time to take ownership of your power in the bedroom.

- Continue to add variety to your sex life. For example, if he loved it when you tied his hands together with silk ties, offer to let him tie you up next time.
- Send him a text message during the day with a teaser for what you plan to do to him that night.
- Surprise him by waking him up with oral sex.

What not to say and do

Charles Bukowski described perfectly described how your partner feels about this sexual experience when he said, "Sexual intercourse is kicking death in the ass while singing." After such an experience, the worst thing you can do is go back to the drudgery of rote lovemaking.

- Don't think of this explosive sexual experience as a "fluke."
- Don't fall back on old habits. Ride the momentum of the sexual energy you created by introducing something new—a different toy, position, etc.— every few times you have sex with your partner.

How both of you will benefit

Couples that have frequent, satisfying sex are more affectionate and empathetic toward their partners. They also just like each other more. The *Elle*/MSNBC.com survey found that 97 percent of the men and women who said they were "very satisfied" with their sex lives also reported having a great relationship with their partner. They attributed this in part to good communication and to "openness to trying new tricks" in the bedroom.

Checklist for Action

- Send your partner a text that says, "You are in for it tonight!"
- Lay out 2 nighties in the morning and ask him which he wants to come home to.
- Leave a blindfold on his pillow as a symbol that he cannot anticipate what you will do next.

How to Handle Impotence

He is deeply humiliated when
he cannot get an erection.

The Scenario
You usually have a fantastic sex life. But lately, your guy has had trouble getting an erection. He refuses to talk about it and is so embarrassed that he has lost interest in any form of sexual contact. You want to help him because you don't want him to feel so horrible and so you can have your old sex life back.

Situation at a Glance
- He has trouble getting and keeping an erection.
- You think he is no longer attracted to you.
- He does not want to discuss it.
- You suggest he speak to a doctor or therapist.
- He refuses to seek professional help and gets mad at you for suggesting it.
- You want your sex life back and don't want your

husband to feel like he is a failure.

The problem in this situation
Approximately 30 million men in the U.S. suffer from impotence—85 percent of these have an underlying physical cause for the problem. In other words, your husband's problem may be not be psychological. He should see a doctor for a check-up. Certain medications, smoking, heart disease, diabetes, prostate issues, and several other conditions may be causing his impotence. If not, then stress may be to blame. A 2006 study published on BBCNews.com reports that work-related stress caused 15 percent of men to suffer from diminished sex drive, while 5 percent said it made them completely impotent.

What he really means & what he really needs
Erectile dysfunction is an extremely sensitive subject for men. If your partner could crawl into a dark hole and never come out, he probably would. He needs you to help him feel comfortable enough to bring the problem to light so he can start dealing with it.

What you need to say and do
Heart of Darkness author Joseph Conrad wrote, "Being a woman is a terribly difficult task, since it consists

principally in dealing with men." Indeed, there are few issues as difficult as impotence for a couple to deal with. It is particularly treacherous for you because you don't understand the causes, mechanics, or emotional impact it has on your husband. The best way to handle the problem is to break it down into manageable parts.

- Get educated. Many books, articles, and Web sites are dedicated to erectile dysfunction. The more you know, the better equipped you will be to support your partner both in and out of the bedroom.
- Make it about "us." Whenever you discuss your partner's impotence, use "we" and "us" instead of "you." Such as, "I think we should see a doctor." Phrasing it that way establishes that you plan to attack the problem as a team.
- Keep kissing, touching, and cuddling your husband.

What not to say and do
Don't make the problem about you: What did I do wrong? Why isn't he attracted to me? When you turn the spotlight onto yourself, you increase your partner's guilt about his condition. This is too much responsibility for most men to handle.

- Don't force him to discuss his impotence after a

failed attempt to get or maintain an erection. Give him time to recover his pride first.

- Don't be a bully. You may be tempted to use threats to get him to seek help. But threatening to get your needs met elsewhere will only hurt him and make the problem worse.

How both of you will benefit

Though your partner views his problem as personal and embarrassing, your support is essential. Navigating this issue as a team will strengthen your marriage bond. It also proves that no issue is too tough for your marriage to handle.

Questions to Ask Your Partner

- Do you want me to make a doctor's appointment for you?
- Do you want me to go with you to the doctor?
- Can I share with you what I've learned about erectile dysfunction?
- Did you know that erectile dysfunction is highly treatable?

Tips &
Exercises

Use the following activities,
tips and advice to enhance your
sex and intimacy.

Three Steps to a Better Orgasm ... For Him

He thrives on spontaneity, variety, and a combination of
tenderness and rough, raunchy sex. Drive him wild by
introducing the following ideas into your sex life when
he least expects it.

Step 1: Wake him up with good morning oral sex.

In an *Elle* magazine and MSNBC.com poll, 58 percent
of women admitted they don't like performing oral sex.
As a result, most men don't expect their partner to go
down on them unless it's a special occasion. Make him
feel like it's his birthday with good morning oral sex a
few times.

Step 2: Include his whole package in the fun.

Women rarely pay attention to a man's testicles during sex. But with the right amount of pressure from the hand or mouth, gently fondling his testes during hand or oral stimulation will greatly increase the intensity of his orgasm.

Step 3: Tease, move, and dominate.

Playfully dominate your partner by refusing to allow him to completely enter your vagina or mouth until you say so. Tease the shaft of his penis with your lubricated hand or tongue for as long as he can stand it. When you finally allow him to enter you, expect an explosive orgasm!

Appearance & Health

In 2006, General Motors aired a commercial advertising the Hummer H3. The ad featured two men in a check-out line at a grocery store. As the first man's vegetables and tofu were rung up by the cashier, he looked self-consciously at the stack of steak, ribs, beef jerky, and charcoal that the "real man" behind him was about to purchase.

After gazing at a Hummer ad in a magazine, the tofu-eating guy rushes from the market to a car dealership and buys a Hummer as a way of regaining his manhood. In fact, the original title of the commercial was "Restore Your Manhood." Though Hummer later cowed to criticism and changed the title to "Restore the Balance," the message of the commercial rang loud and clear: big meat plus big car equals big manhood.

Men are constantly assaulted by such messages that tell them being a real man involves making certain dietary choices. These usually include eschewing anything green, howling like an animal at dead meat and barbecue, and guzzling beer and soda as if it were going out of style. Advertisers seek to capitalize on the prominent notion that eating healthy is for sissies. As *Advertising Age* columnist Bob Garfield says of this tactic, "A Double Whopper becomes a badge of masculinity regained."

Figure out why he does what he does:

1. He eats the way men are taught to eat.

2. He exercises mainly to bond with other men or to blow off steam, but not primarily to improve his health.

3. He is oblivious to minor changes in your appearance, but terrified of major ones, such as cosmetic surgery or radical haircuts.

Indeed, your partner's sense of self is, in large part, defined by billions of dollars in advertisements. These ads establish and reinforce the idea that eating a 1,000-calorie cheeseburger that has 32 grams of fat (plus fries and a milkshake!) establishes masculinity, restores pride, and asserts independence in a world that is constantly trying to take his manhood away from him.

As you navigate the appearance and health challenges that crop up in your relationship, keep these assaults in mind. In the same way that women have been the lifelong target of advertisers who seek to sell them diet and beauty products, so too has your partner been on the receiving end of a campaign to link his masculinity with his diet. The following chapter will show you how to help him divorce his masculinity from a traditionally masculine diet, and address other health and appearance issues that crop up.

Help Him Love Eating Healthy

He needs a reminder that
good health takes effort.

The Scenario

The only time your partner wears workout clothes is
to sit on the couch and watch TV and eat frozen pizza
and chicken wings. You want to encourage him to get
back to the gym because he's developing a large gut and
you're worried about his health. You don't want to nag
him or hurt his feelings, but something has to be done
because you're less attracted to him and want to do
activities together.

Situation at a Glance

- You are worried about your husband's health.
- He likes to eat junk food and relax instead of
  working out.
- You are less attracted to him in his unhealthy state.
- He is easily winded and doesn't want to have sex
  as often.

- You are grossed out by his diet.
- He says he just wants to do his own thing.

The problem in this situation

Your partner's bachelor diet turns you off now that you're in a serious relationship. You thought you would be able to train him to eat right, but it's not working. He loves all food, including fresh fruits and vegetables, but he drenches them in butter and salt, and usually eats them alongside fried chicken or steak. You are concerned about his health and grossed out by his post-meal greasy fingers and mouth, but you don't want to come across as a nag or make him feel bad.

What he really means & what he really needs

Your husband thinks that because he eats fruits and vegetables with most of his meals that his diet is well-balanced—maybe even healthy. Like many of the 103.7 million overweight or obese men in America, he doesn't think his diet is a problem. He also doesn't make the connection between his high-fat diet and lack of exercise and sluggish behavior and decreased sex drive. He needs you to help him see that good nutrition and regular exercise results in good health and more energy.

What you need to say and do

Gently, tell your husband his diet is causing a rift in your relationship. In addition to missing out on sharing the same kinds of dishes, the extra calories in his are making him look not as good as you think he could. Tell him you love him and want to make healthy eating easy and enjoyable for him.

- Make veggies as easy to grab as chips by keeping chopped carrots, celery, jicama, and other fresh, crunchy vegetables in the fridge for snacking. Pair with peanut butter, salsa, hummus, cottage cheese, or mashed avocado for dipping.
- Cook healthy dinners and eat at the table most nights. Feature several kinds of foods (i.e., a soup, a salad, a side dish, a protein, and even a healthy dessert) so he feels he has plenty of interesting tastes to choose from.
- Send your husband an email to remind him that you packed his lunch to discourage him from getting fast food.

What not to say and do

As much as you want to help your husband eat better, it is not your job to be the food police. Besides, he will be much more agreeable to your dietary suggestions if you don't call him out every time he eats something that is unhealthy.

- Don't ask him to use nonfat yogurt while you load up your baked potato with butter and sour cream.
- Don't humiliate him with insults like, "You eat like a pig!" or, "Don't you think you've had enough?"
- Don't expect him to change his eating habits overnight.
- Avoid overloading him with diet facts, cookbooks, and healthy alternatives. Just limit his choices by stocking only healthy ingredients.

How both of you will benefit

Eating a low-fat, high-fiber diet in conjunction with regular exercise reduces risk of death from heart disease, cancer, and diabetes. Committing to a healthier lifestyle also provides an energy boost, improves mood and self-esteem, and effectively jumpstarts a stalled sex drive.

Things to Help Your Partner Realize

- Eating 20 to 35 grams of fiber per day decreases the risk of developing colon cancer by 40 percent.
- Men who exercise regularly are less likely to suffer from erectile dysfunction.

Help Him
Notice You

He may not notice when you
change your appearance, but it doesn't
mean he doesn't care.

The Scenario
Your new haircut makes you feel gorgeous, and it seems like everyone except for your husband loves it! He never notices when you change your appearance and rarely pays you any compliments. You're sick of it and feel taken for granted.

Situation at a Glance
- You want to know that he thinks you are pretty.
- He doesn't notice when you get your hair cut.
- You think because he doesn't notice, he doesn't care.
- He doesn't expect you to notice every little change he makes to his look.
- You worry he is so used to you that he can't even see you anymore.
- He feels ambushed by your expectations.

The problem in this situation

You walk out of the salon feeling glamorous and like a brand-new woman. But it's a buzz kill when your partner doesn't notice, and you are quickly reduced to feeling frumpy and invisible. He doesn't notice your haircut because he's like the majority of American men—oblivious.

What he really means & what he really needs

According to a 2009 AXE survey about hair, only 29 percent of men think hair is an important consideration for attracting a partner. And once he's got you, he still doesn't think it matters. Subtle haircuts to add layers or trim a few inches off the bottom won't catch his eye because for the most part he's focused on your face, eyes, lips, and body.

What you need to say and do

Take the pressure off of the situation by immediately making the following announcement, "I love my new haircut! It makes me feel so pretty!" He'll get that he's supposed to agree, you'll get a compliment, and you will both benefit from your straightforwardness.

- Give him a heads up—with reminders—whenever you plan to make a change to your appearance. Tell him that morning, "I'm getting my hair cut and colored later today." Then after your appointment, send him a text that reads, "My hair turned out great! I hope it knocks your socks off when I see you later."

- Forget waiting for him to come up with his own compliments. Be bold and tell him what you want to hear. Say something like, "When I buy a new outfit, get a haircut, or change my look, it would make me feel great if you noticed and told me that you liked it." He'll appreciate the guidance.

What not to say and do

Don't test him to see if he is paying attention to changes in your appearance. It sets an emotional trap that neither of you can get out of without a fight.

- Avoid ambushing him with statements like, "Notice anything different about me?" Chances are he'll have no idea what's different, take a shot in the dark, and be wrong. Just tell him!
- Don't brag about the compliments other men have given you to elicit a response. Making him feel jealous will not inspire him to compliment you.

- Don't have unrealistic expectations for your partner's response. Think about how he reacts to other things—does he ever gush about anything?

How both of you will benefit

Taking charge of your needs and relaying them to your partner reduces the tension in your home. You no longer have to wait for him to notice because you tell him when to notice. Taking the guesswork out of how to compliment you also frees your partner from the trappings of your expectations.

Things to Realize
- Don't take everything so seriously.
- He may not notice your haircut because he's too busy looking at your boobs!
- Give him a chance to succeed by being straightforward.

Motivate Him to Look Great

He dresses down because he
feels safe and settled.

The Scenario

When you were dating he dressed up and sharply, and always smelled great. Now that you are married, it's like he doesn't care how he looks—or smells. You love him no matter what he looks like, but lately you've been nostalgic for the days when you were proud to be that smartly dressed couple that turned other peoples' heads.

Situation at a Glance
- You miss when your partner put effort into his appearance.
- He dresses for comfort these days.
- On the weekends you can barely get him to take a shower, let along wear cologne.
- He saves dressing up and wearing cologne for special occasions.

- You think he has gotten too comfortable—and lazy.
- He thinks one of the benefits of marriage is that you get to stop having to impress your partner.

The problem in this situation

There is an old joke that goes, "Love is blind, but marriage is an eye-opener." It wasn't until you were married that you realized your partner's style was actually just his wooing costume. Now that you're officially his, there is no reason for him to keep up his A game. He won the prize—you! He is happy, comfortable, and ready to retire his quest to be best dressed in your eyes.

What he really means & what he really needs

The first time his dressed down look went unnoticed, it was like he got permission to live in sweat pants. Men are habit-forming creatures of comfort. Given the choice between khakis and cargoes, he'll go with the cargoes every time. He needs you to step in and help him make changes to his style.

What you need to say and do

Mark Twain once quipped, "Clothes make the man. Naked people have little or no influence on society." If your partner's outfits around the house reflect his influence in the home, he might as well be naked! Help him regain his rightful place by dressing him up without tearing him down. Men are visual learners and fashion followers—so show him how you want him to dress by taking an active role in building his closet.

- Tell him you want to spoil him with a shopping trip for being such a great husband. When he declines, say, "Okay, I will shop for you then!"
- Sneak new outfits into his closet.
- When you see a nice shirt on another man, exclaim, "I think you'd look really good in that shirt!"
- Tell him when he wears cologne all you can think about is making love with him.

What not to say and do

Don't perform last rites on your husband's fashion sense just yet. Everyone goes through "comfortable" phases, and so it's likely his style is not dead—but rather it just needs resuscitation.

- Don't expect him to change willingly from sweats to slacks. Give him incentives to step up his style. For example, plan a dinner at nice restaurant with friends and let him know that everyone will be dressing up.

- Don't be above using sex to bribe him. Let him know you are turned on when he looks nice. Then reward him with great sex whenever he matches your fashion expectations.

How both of you will benefit

Chances are your partner slipped into his fashion coma so slowly he didn't even notice it happen. It is also probably exacerbated by an incipient weight gain: A 2007 study published in *USA Today* reports that couples gain an average of 15 to 30 pounds within 5 years of getting married. Revive his desire to look and feel great by rewarding him with affection and sexual gratification instead of by nagging or with insults. Indeed, good health and good self-esteem are both part of a good marriage.

Questions to Ask Yourself

- Do my expectations for how I want my partner to dress match the effort I put in to my appearance?
- Could there be a serious reason for my partner's disinterest in his appearance, such as depression or illness?

Always Be the One He Loves

He takes dramatic changes to your appearance as a sign that you are gearing up to start a new life—without him.

The Scenario

Over dinner you tell your partner you are ready for a complete makeover and that you are considering cosmetic surgery. He responds by predicting you will leave him with a year of having surgery and begs you to reconsider. You are shocked by his response and want to reassure him this is not the case. You think this will increase your self-esteem and make you happier, not make you want to leave him.

Situation at a Glance

- You want to enhance your appearance with cosmetic surgery.
- He believes once you have surgery, you will leave him.
- You want to do this for you, not for him or any other man.

- He equates your dissatisfaction with your appearance with you being unhappy with him.
- You need him to be supportive.
- He can't see beyond his own fears.

The problem in this situation

Your partner's fears are not necessarily unfounded. A *Grazia* magazine study discovered that up to 40 percent of women who undergo cosmetic surgery do end up leaving their partners—even when they pay for the procedure! Women that ditch their partners post-op experience a turbo-boost in self-confidence when they finally feel like their appearance matches their state-of-mind. Some women cannot resist finding out what life is like as their new and improved selves, and this is what your partner is afraid of.

What he really means & what he really needs

Contrary to what you believe, your partner is not opposed to your quest for self-improvement. He would wholeheartedly support you in gradual efforts to improve your health and appearance, such as developing an exercise routine, changing your diet, quitting smoking, or reducing alcohol and caffeine consumption. What makes cosmetic surgery different and scary is that it is instant, dramatic, and risky.

What you need to say and do

Thoroughly discuss the pros and cons of plastic surgery with your partner. And as you weigh them, dig deep and be honest with yourself about why you want to surgically alter your appearance.

- According to the *Grazia* study, 64 percent of women hoped having surgery would increase their self-confidence, 42 percent hoped to look younger, and 13 percent admitted they wanted men to notice them.
- Demystify your motives by including him every step of the way. He will feel less insecure if he is allowed to participate in activities such as sitting in on consultations.

What not to say and do

Don't delude yourself about any of the possible physical, social, and emotional ramifications of having cosmetic surgery. Even if that means saying out loud, "We can't know what will happen afterwards." Take the straightforward, honest approach, even when it's difficult.

- Don't ignore safety to save a buck. *Glamour* magazine reports the American Society for

Dermatologic Surgery has seen complications from cosmetic surgery done by low-cost, non-specialists rise steadily since 2005.

- Don't have work done—even small procedures—without discussing it with your partner. It will feed his insecurities and cause him to feel betrayed.

How both of you will benefit

When something as big as cosmetic surgery is plopped onto the dinner table, it is time to team up and attack the issue from all sides. Hiding post-op divorce statistics or denying the health risks involved will not reduce his insecurities. However, researching and discussing all of the pros and cons with your partner takes him along—as far as is possible—on your journey, which makes it less threatening.

Checklist for Action

- Share all of your research with your partner.
- Interview prospective doctors with your husband.
- Admit to all of the reasons motivating you to change your appearance.

Tips & Exercises

Use the following activities,
tips and advice to enhance your discussions
about appearance and health.

He Wants You to Look and Feel Your Best

In some relationships, it is the woman who lets her appearance slide. Perhaps when you and your husband dated you spent an hour getting ready to go out. But now that you're married, it feels silly to dress up for him, even though he thinks you stopped dressing up because you stopped caring. Or, perhaps your partner encourages you to go to the gym with such enthusiasm that you are starting to think he is disgusted with your appearance. It's not that, but he wants you to look and feel your best, too. Here's why:

- Heart disease is the leading cause of death for women.

Your partner wants to live a long, healthy, problem-free life with you! Risk of cardiac-related death can be greatly reduced by eating low-calorie, low-fat, high-fiber diet and by exercising regularly at moderate intensity.

- Women who like the way they look have higher self-esteem than those who don't.

Women with high self-esteem are generally more pleasant to be around—their confidence and charm can be magnetic. Furthermore, women with high self-esteem are more likely to leave the lights on during sex or be willing to try new positions.

- He is most attracted to you when you look and feel your best.

Taking care of your physical and emotional well-being causes you to exude confidence and command self-respect, qualities he finds irresistible. Also, dressing up for him makes him feel special and lucky to have secured this beautiful woman as his life-long partner.

Conclusion

Hopefully, reading *The Ultimate Guide for Women to Understand Men* has helped you realize that understanding your husband or boyfriend's behavior, though challenging at times, is entirely possible.

You should have come to understand that the way his family, peers, and even society have trained him to maintain a relationship has been very different from yours. As a result he is prone to different reactions and expectations, and it is best to work to understand them rather than try to change them. With this book at your disposal, you will be able to eliminate much of the guesswork involved in figuring out why he thinks a relationship can run on autopilot.

Moreover, you should feel more in control of your relationship, because this book has shown you many ways you can grab the reins on your own reactions, behaviors, and assumptions. Using real-life scenarios to deconstruct how couples deal with commitment, communication, priorities and values, money, sex, and health issues has likely taught you to deal with a multitude of issues on an individual level. You have also learned how to handle your partner's expectations by implementing well-researched suggestions for what to do—and what not to do—in various realistic situations. In addition, you now understand that backing off is sometimes the best path to conflict resolution. Finally, you have learned that the six major components of a relationship may not require as much maintenance as you used to think.

Armed with the hope that your relationship is not permanently disabled by the drudgery of everyday life, you should feel inspired to employ the hundreds of concrete methods for improving your relationship contained within these pages. Indeed, doing so is sure to reinvigorate your emotional connection with your partner as well as reignite the spark in the life you share together.